Zany Rainy Days

Indoor Ideas for Active Kids

Hallie Warshaw

with Mark Shulman

Photography by Morten Kettel

Sterling Publishing Co., Inc.
New York

Zany Rainy Days

Creative Director
Hallie Warshaw

Photographer
Morten Kettel

Head Writer
Mark Shulman

Head Activity Writers
Belena Raisin
Jake Miller

Graphic Designers
Hallie Warshaw
Tanya Napier

Editor
Robyn Brode

Production Artist
Doug Popovich

Illustrator
Kris Bhat

Creative Assistant
Tanya Napier

Photoshoot Assistants
Chris Mitchell
Kris Bhat

Library of Congress Cataloging-in-Publication Data

Warshaw, Hallie.
  Zany rainy days : indoor ideas for active kids / Hallie Warshaw ;
photography by Morten Kettel.
    p. cm.
  Includes index.
  ISBN 0-8069-6623-8
  1. Indoor games. 2. Creative activities and seat work. I. Title.

GV1229 .W33 2000
793--dc21

10 9 8 7 6 5 4 3 2 1

Published by Sterling Publishing Company, Inc.
387 Park Avenue South, New York, NY 10016

Created and produced by Orange Avenue, Inc.
275 Fifth Street, San Francisco, CA 94103, USA

Distributed in Canada by Sterling Publishing Co., Inc.
c/o Canadian Manda Group, One Atlantic Avenue, Suite 105
Toronto, Ontario, Canada M6K 3E7

Distributed in Great Britain and Europe by Chris Lloyd
463 Ashley Road, Parkstone, Poole, Dorset
BH14 0AX, England

Distributed in Australia by Capricorn Link (Australia) Pty Ltd.
P.O. Box 6651, Baulkham Hills, Business Centre NSW 2153, Australia

Sterling ISBN 0-8069-6623-8

Created by

Orange Avenue

Making Creative Products for Growing Minds

San Francisco • New York

If you would like to correspond with us, send an email with your favorite rainy-day projects to umbrellahead@zanyrainydays.com.

THANK YOU... IT TAKES A LOT OF PEOPLE TO MAKE A BOOK!

Thanks goes to everyone who participated in the creation, execution, and production of this book. We couldn't have done it without all of you!

CHILDREN MODELS

Virginia Babasa
Justin Baker Rhett
Zane Baker Rhett
Carolyn L. E. Bazen
Maggie Belshaw
Surya Bhat
Dyantha Burton
Julia Burton
Hannah Lei Byers-Straus
Arnold Joseph Cabuang
Maya Ruth Cameron

Lea Chernock
Sophia Durning
Hank Foo
Gabrielle Fusco-Rodriguez
Mario Fusco-Rodriguez
Ana Guerrero
Leslie Hession
Zachariah Ho Seher
Zoe Ho Seher
Asia Lynn Jamison
Alex Koka

Nathalie Koka
Beth Matteucci
Will Matteucci
Katrina McGraw
Ethan Merrill
Samantha Moran-Rodriguez
Perry Marie Naimark Shadwick
Lucia Oberste-Hufft
Dominic Parker Butler
Nicolas Parker Butler
Erin Price-Dickson

Corinna Ricard-Farzan
Jess Robbins
Naomi Clara Robin
Christopher Scally
Thomas Scally
Emiko Shimabukuro
John Springer
Maria Vicencio
Terri Washington
Marcus Wells
Adam Wojewidka

Special thanks to Blossom Matteucci, the dog, and to the parents and grown-ups for all the carpools, tips, and support for this project!

ACTIVITIES

Belena Raisin
Bowwow Biscuits
Crazy Corn-Chip Chili
Delicious Dirt Pies
Fancy Frames
Fantastic Hats
Instrument Maker
Italian Pizza Buns
Lip-Synch Singer
Mexican Piñata
News Reporter
Presto! Magic Wands
Recycling Bins

Show Producer
Smushy Smoothies
Song Rewriter
Stand-up Comedian
Sunshine Cupcakes
Superstar Iced Cookies
Surprise Collage Cards
Write a Politician

Jake Miller
African Bead Necklaces
Attractive Magnet Frames
Carnaval Mystery Masks

Concentration Cards
Fame Game
Flashlight Monsters
Hallway Bowling
Japanese Origami Butterflies
Native American Button Blankets
Pioneer Pot Holders
Puppeteer
Puppy Puppet Maker
Scary Storytelling
Sock Soccer
Spanish Paper Mosaics
Super Scavenger Hunt
Wild Animal Limbo

Lily Byers
Continuous Calendar

Kris Bhat
Bug Dice
Sole Mates

Alex Mace
Nutty Noodle People
Tabletop Football
Velcro Target Ball

Tanya Napier
Shapely Beanbags
Unfolding Stories

PHOTOSHOOT HOMES

Thank you for letting us use your homes: the Byers family, Ho Seher family, Bhat family, Koka family, and Matteucci family.

SPECIAL THANKS

Charles Nurnberg, Frances Gilbert, Sheila Barry, Bob Warshaw, Rosanne Roberts, Connie Johnson, The Renaissance Entrepreneurship Center, San Francisco.

Contents

make helping fun

chapter **4**

chapter **5**

color away the gray

around the world

chapter **6**

Contents

Read this book and you'll wish you lived in a rain forest.

Okay, so you've got the book on *Zany Rainy Days* in your hands and it isn't raining. What are you going to do about it? Some kids zip up yellow raincoats just before using this book. Some kids open every umbrella in the house and then sit under them, on the rug, planning their projects. Some kids turn on a whole system of high-powered garden hoses over every window, and play thunder tapes, and use lightning lamps, and, yes, those kids are definitely out of control. But some kids know the secret…

YOU DON'T NEED RAIN!

The projects in *Zany Rainy Days* will actually work inside, outside, side by side, and inside out. But if you don't need rain, what *do* you need? You need this book. You need supplies. You need a brain that works (mostly). And you need to like doing stuff that's fun. If you don't like having fun, we have another book for you. It's called the phone book—just read it until the clouds go away.

AMAZING FACTS!

According to scientists, 4 out of 5 people under the age of 94 need help having fun on a rainy day. If you're one of the people who sits in front of a TV or computer every time the rain clouds crash, this book can help save your eyeballs. You'll make things you can be proud of, maybe even help people, and when the sun comes out you won't have to squint!

TAKE THE PLEDGE

You're not a wimpy complainer when rain takes outdoor play away, are you? (No.) YOU know how to have good fun in bad weather, right? (Yes.) To prove it, just take the *Zany Rainy Days* pledge:

THE ZANY RAINY DAYS PLEDGE

Raise your left hand and say this out loud in front of people:

I [say your name] am NOT a wimpy complainer. I have a good imagination. I can have fun while huge buckets of water pour down from the sky. I can have fun without sitting and staring at a screen. I can have fun without breaking things. I can have fun without hiding under the bed. I know how to have fun... just like the early pioneers, if they had a book like this, and art supplies, and didn't have to worry about bears all the time. And that's the truth.

(You can put your hand down now.)

You can survive anything...

It's raining. It's pouring. And this is the page where we're supposed to give you the usual warnings. You know…about being clean instead of messy, and quiet instead of loud, and smart instead of dumb.

But forget it. You won't read that stuff anyway. Why should you? You're a KID! Someone would have to tie you to a lightning rod to make you listen to safety rules.

Who cares if you burn yourself in the kitchen? Burns feel good, right? (Wrong.) **Who cares** if you lose a finger? They grow back, right? (Wrong.) **Who cares** if you eat crayons and drink paint—you'll look really colorful at your funeral, right? (Wrong, unless you're inside out.)

And who cares if running all over the house drives adults crazy? They'll just laugh at the noise and the mess and all the stuff you break, and they'll invite all your friends back next time, right? (Are you kidding?)

Let's not even try to warn you. If you're klutzy enough to wreck the house…if you're dopey enough to let anything touch lightbulbs or to fool with electricity…if your brain is missing the part that's careful around sharp objects…if you're so far gone you think it's okay to get paint and markers on people's furniture…good luck. No one is ever going to let you into their house when it's raining. **You'll get pneumonia** pounding on the door. **And someone else will get your toys.** Is that what you want? So just play smart.

KITCHEN COOKING SAFETY

Here are some rules to follow (and what to expect if you don't):

1. Read the entire recipe before you begin. Find the ingredients and utensils first, and have them ready to use. Or you'll get a free membership to Mistakes-R-Us.

2. Wash your hands before cooking and eating. Or you'll meet your friendly Poison Control Team.

3. Use pot holders when handling hot dishes on top of the stove or in the oven. Or you'll have to join the Wyoming Cattle Branding Club.

4. Tie your hair back, if you can. Or you'll get clipped by the Emergency Haircut Squad.

5. Clean up whatever you use. Or you'll have to take a gray bus to the Sloppy Kids Reform School.

6. Don't leave food cooking unattended in the oven or on the stove. Or you might get carried away by the Fire Department's Idiot Disposal Unit.

7. Make sure an adult is nearby. Or best run to the Travelers' Club for a map of faraway, tiny islands.

Emergency gear for every kind of weather

RAINY-DAY TOOLS

The projects in this book use lots of stuff. You might already have some of this stuff. The rest of the stuff is at a store. But if you already have all this stuff, your house is probably stuffed.

- Poster board
- Construction paper
- Cardboard pieces
- Tempera paints
- Brushes
- Markers
- Felt-tipped pens
- Aluminum foil
- Rope and string
- Toothpicks
- Boxes
- Flashlights
- Dice
- Balloons
- Tennis balls
- Tube socks
- Plastic bottles
- Popsicle sticks
- Clothespins
- Poles and sticks

- Dried pasta and rice
- Glitter
- Pom-poms
- Feathers
- Shells and nuts
- Pipe cleaners
- Yarn
- White glue
- Fabric and felt
- Fabric glue
- Velcro
- Buttons and beads
- Sequins
- Ribbons and bows
- Needle and thread
- Safety pins
- Tape measure

- Old clothes
- Old hats
- Old shoes
- Old anything
- CDs and tapes
- Boombox
- Songbooks
- Sheets and blankets
- Tables, chairs, sofa
- Brooms
- Kitchen with ingredients, pots and pans, and pot holders
- Writing paper
- Pens and pencils
- Index cards
- Stapler and ruler
- Hole punch
- Paper glue
- Stickers and labels
- Paper clips and tacks
- Rubber bands
- Newspapers
- Magazines
- Scissors
- Cellophane tape

RAINY-DAY KEYS

Two kinds of keys are useful on a rainy day. The keys below help you select an activity. The keys in your pocket get you indoors when it's raining. Without either one, you're all wet!

If you can read this, you're old enough to do everything in this book. But if you're too young to read this book, why are you? Kids age 6 and up can make any of these activities easier or more challenging—just ask any nearby adult. And if you don't have a nearby adult, find one.

How many people? Except for games requiring at least two players, everything in this book can be enjoyed alone or with whoever is stuck in the house with you.

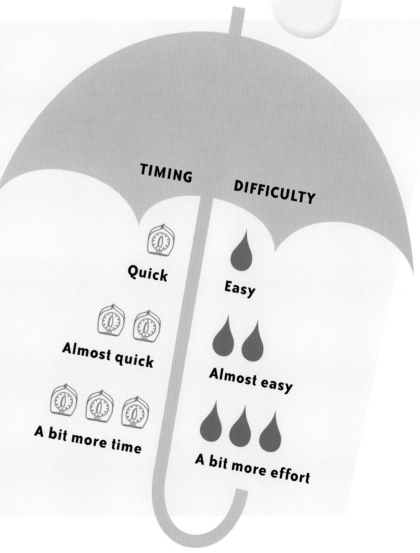

TIMING

Quick

Almost quick

A bit more time

DIFFICULTY

Easy

Almost easy

A bit more effort

rained-out games

When down come the raindrops
You can still have a ball
It can roll into bowling pins
Or bounce off a wall

Play football on tables
Start scavenger hunts
Or dance like an animal
Grunting great grunts

Which games are the best?
The grown-ups don't care
Just as long as your games
Keep you out of their hair!

rained-out games

velcro target ball

Now you can finally throw things in the house! We're talking about Velcro Target Ball. Follow these simple instructions and you'll be playing in no time. Practice by yourself or play with some friends.

Medium-sized roll of self-sticking Velcro

Large piece of cardboard

2 ping-pong balls

Magic marker

Tape or Velcro

Notepad and pencil

here's how...

1. Draw four to six concentric circles on a large piece of cardboard or poster board. The center circle is the bull's-eye and should be about the size of a piece of salami.

2. Decide how many points each circle should earn. Using the margic marker, write the smallest number in the largest circle. Write the next smallest number in the next largest, and so on, until you get to the smallest one. The bull's-eye is the hardest one to hit, so it should be worth the most points.

3. Cut lots of pieces of Velcro about 1 inch long from one side of the roll of Velcro, and space them evenly within each circle, sticking on as many as you like. The larger the spaces between the pieces, the harder the game will be, because the balls will have fewer pieces of Velcro on which to stick.

4. Mount the target on a wall with tape.

5. Using the leftover side of Velcro, cut out four strips about 4 inches long. They should be as wide as the Velcro roll.

6. Wrap one of the strips tightly around a ping-pong ball, sticking the ends of the Velcro together. Wrap another strip diagonally, to cover the rest of the ball, and stick the ends together.

7. Do the same with the other ping-pong ball.

8. Stand about 10 feet away and try to hit the Velcro pieces in the target circles with the ping-pong balls. A direct hit should cause the ball to stick to the target. Each player gets to throw both balls each turn.

9. When a ping-pong ball sticks to the target, the player should write down the number of points earned on a scorecard.

10. Add up a player's score at the end of each turn. The first player to get 150 points wins!

How hard

How long

rained-out games

hallway bowling

Want to take bowling up to the next level, and down your own hallway? In this game, pinball meets miniature golf. Just set 'em up and knock 'em down—and you won't even bust the walls!

here's how...

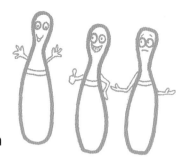

1. First, set up your "bowling alley." Get three to ten empty, clean plastic drink bottles. They're your pins. At one end of the hallway, set up the pins in a triangle. Make sure that the pins are close enough together so that when the first one falls over it will knock the others down, too.

2. For the "bowling balls," use tennis balls, squash balls, or any mix of similar bouncy balls.

3. At the very end of the hall, lay out the blanket to keep your bowling balls from rolling too far away.

4. Each bowler gets three turns. When you've used up all three balls, count how many pins you've knocked over. Then set them up for the next player.

5. Start simply. Try bowling straight down the lane a few times until you get the hang of knocking the pins down. Then try bouncing the ball off the walls, so it ricochets off the sides of the alley.

6. After everyone has had a turn, you can rebuild the alley. Try adding a few obstacles—shoes, cushions, books, and so forth—to the hallway. Now you have to make your ball bounce around them on its way to the pins.

7. You can also build ramps to get the ball up and over some of the obstacles. Just prop a piece of cardboard up on a phone book or a shoe, and you're ready to fly.

How hard

How long

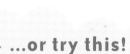

...or try this!

You don't need a hard floor to bowl on; bowling also works on a rug. Use a pair of rolled-up tube socks for the ball. Be sure to *roll* the ball. It's not as easy as it seems!

rained-out games

wild animal limbo

If you want to dance the limbo, you have to bend over backward! Everybody loves to limbo—even wild animals. Go wild yourself, use your imagination, and see just how low you can go!

here's how...

1. The object of limbo dancing is to see who can dance under a "limbo bar" the most times without touching it. A limbo bar is a broomstick, rope, or string.

2. Two people can hold the limbo bar while the others dance under it, one by one. Everyone should take turns holding the bar. You can also tie the rope to a door handle or prop the bar on boxes or chairs, so that no one has to hold it. Make sure you leave enough room on each side so you can get your arms under the bar.

3. The dancers should choose an animal and then try to go underneath the bar like that animal would. Birds should flap their wings, elephants should swing their trunks, frogs should hop, and so on. No fair copying other people's animals, and no fair doing the same animal twice. (But if one person wants to be a cobra and another wants to be a rattlesnake, that's okay.)

4. Every time the whole group has made it under, make the bar a little lower. Dancers who touch or bump the bar, or lose their balance and fall over, are out of the contest.

5. As the bar gets lower, try to think of animals that move low to the ground. Save the lowest—like a crab, a lizard, or a snake—for when the bar gets really low.

6. The winner is the one who can go the lowest and still get under the bar.

...or try this!

Choose someone to be in charge of playing your favorite music while everyone else dances and play-acts being an animal. When the "disk jockey" stops the music, the "animals" have to freeze in animal poses until the music starts up again.

How hard

How long

rained-out games

sock soccer

what you need

Pair of tube socks

Towel

Clock or watch

Even if it's raining out, you can still play soccer. You don't need a field, a ball, a goal, or a minivan to get the team there. Get yourself an extra pair of socks and make enough room to kick, pass, and score without getting a furniture-shaped dent in your head!

22

here's how...

1. To make your ball, take a pair of tube socks and roll them up inside each other. Try to make the ball as round as you can, but don't worry if it's a little wobbly. That's part of the fun.

2. Mark off the playing field—as big as the area you'd need for a dance. On one end of the field, lay a towel on the floor a couple of feet away from the wall. That's the goal. To score, you have to kick the ball so that it stays on the towel; if it rolls off or goes past the towel altogether, it's no good. Don't kick too hard!

3. The wall at the other end of the room is the midfield. When the team that is defending the goal kicks the ball back to the midfield wall, it can try to score a goal.

4. Don't get too close! If the attacking team gets near enough to the goal to stretch out and step on it, it has to give up the ball to the other team. If any of the defenders gets close enough to a shooter for the shooter to touch him or her, then the shooting team gets a free kick at the goal, with no blocking allowed. (It's not fair for the shooter to chase the defender just to get a free shot.)

5. Also, of course, team players can't use their hands to touch the ball. If a shooter commits a hand-ball, it's the other team's turn to be offense. If a defender does, the shooters get a free shot at the goal.

6. At the end of 5 minutes, if no one has scored or kicked the ball back to midfield, it's time to switch sides.

...or try this!

Use a human goalie. Assign one person to be the goalkeeper, who sits on the ground and behind the goal. The goalie can touch the ball with his or her hands or head to keep it off the towel.

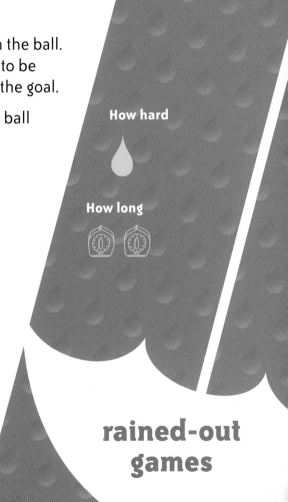

How hard

How long

rained-out games

tabletop football

Whenever you can't play football outside, it's time to play Tabletop Football! Using only one piece of paper, you and a friend can score touchdowns, field goals, and extra points all day, without even leaving the table.

Here's how to make a tabletop football:

1.

2.

3.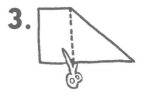

4.

5.

6.

7.
Tape

here's how...

making the football

The illustrations on the opposite page show the seven easy steps to make a football using paper, scissors, and tape.

playing the game

The two football players sit on opposite sides of the table. The object is to flick the football across the table with your thumb and forefinger. You get three flicks to get the football hanging over the other player's end of the table without falling off.

scoring

- If you manage to get the football to hang off the other player's end of the table without falling off, you have scored a touchdown, which is worth 6 points.

- If you score a touchdown, you get to try for 1 extra point.

- If you knock the football off the table, the other player gets to try for a field goal, which is worth 3 points.

- The first player to get 35 points wins!

field goals and extra points

- The player who is not kicking: Make two L's with your thumbs and index fingers. Then touch the thumbs together so that you get three sides of a square. Rest your wrists on the table (elbows make it harder). This is called *the uprights*.

- The player who is kicking: To kick field goals and get extra points, hold the football between the table and your index finger. Using your other hand, flick the football using your thumb and middle finger. Try to kick it through the uprights. If it goes through, you get 3 points for a field goal or 1 point for an extra point.

How hard

How long

rained-out games

Paper

Pens or pencils

Treasure sack
or chest

super
scavenger hunt

There's lots of fun hidden around your house.
Know where you can find it? On a scavenger hunt!

here's how...

1. Make a list of treasures to hunt for. Everyone should take turns naming some things to find.

2. Think of things you can find and bring back—like the smallest book or five blue objects. And things that you can find out about—like seeing who can name the most objects in the living room that make noise by themselves. Other good categories of treasures are things like the greenest, shiniest, or sweetest.

3. Decide on the rules: Do you want to work alone or in teams? Are some rooms off-limits? Do you want to make it a race to see who can finish finding everything first, no matter how long it takes? Or do you want to see who can find the most things within a time limit? Do you want to give a prize to the winner?

4. Now that you know what you're hiding and what the rules are, each side needs to make up some clues to help the other players figure out what they'll be hunting for. For example, if one side is hiding a blue comb, the clue might say, "I am blue, but your hair isn't (I hope!)." Or the clue to a tennis ball might simply be, "What is round and green and bouncy?"

5. Let the hunt begin! Find the objects on the list and carry them in your sack, and write down the answers to the questions or riddles on your paper.

6. When the hunt is done, compare your treasures and find out who collected the most. You can't count things you bring back that don't match the clues!

7. Make sure you put everything back where it belongs!

...or try this!

Alphabet hiding is when you hide an object next to something that starts with the same letters. For instance, if you hide the comb under a corn-chip bag, no one may even find it until you make chili!

How hard

How long

Activity link
Turn the page to find out about the chili mentioned in alphabet hiding.

rained-out games

Measuring cups

Measuring spoons

Large stockpot or Dutch oven

Wooden spoon

crazy corn-chip chili

Not only is this the tastiest chili you will ever have, but it's also the most fun to eat! Enjoy this meal just like the pioneers did in the Wild West—right from the little yellow bags!

INGREDIENTS

2 tablespoons olive oil

3/4 cup chopped onions

1 teaspoon salt

3/4 pound ground chuck

1 tablespoon chili powder

2 teaspoons ground cumin

1 teaspoon dried oregano

1 1/2 cups (14 ounces) crushed tomatoes with added puree

2 1/2 cups (20 ounces) low-sodium chicken broth

1/2 cup tomato paste

1 can (15 ounces) prepared pinto beans, drained

6–8 bags (1 1/4 ounces) corn chips

Shredded cheddar cheese

here's how...

1. Heat oil in a heavy stockpot or Dutch oven over medium-high heat.

2. Add onions and salt. Sauté until onions are soft but not brown, about 8 minutes.

3. Add the ground chuck and sauté until brown, breaking up the meat into small pieces with the back of a wooden spoon, about 5 minutes.

4. Add chili powder, cumin, and oregano. Stir for an additional 2 minutes.

5. Mix in the crushed tomatoes, chicken broth, and tomato paste. Simmer for about 25 minutes on low heat, stirring occasionally to prevent the chili from sticking to the bottom of the pan.

6. Mix in beans and simmer for an additional 5 minutes.

7. Using scissors, cut an "X" across the front of 6 to 8 lunchbox-sized bags of corn chips.

8. One at a time, put each bag in a bowl and peel back the corners. Put the chili inside.

9. Add shredded cheese and let it melt a little.

10. Now call your friends "pardner" and sing cowboy songs in your worst campfire voice before digging in.

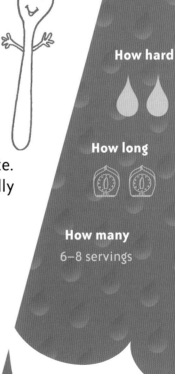

How hard

How long

How many
6–8 servings

rained-out games

outdoors indoors

When you feel like the rain
Is cramping your style
Just ask yourself
Is camping your style?

Build a big fort
With blankets and wire
Bring in the flashlights
But leave out the fire

Sing and tell stories
Make arts and crafts
And if it keeps raining
Learn to build rafts!

outdoors indoors

couch fort

4–5 sheets
and blankets

Lots of pillows

Some shoes

Brooms, mops,
or long sticks

Flashlights

Make a fort using a couch or large chair as the frame and blankets for the sides. Pillows, shoes, long sticks, and brooms will keep the tent from blowing away in case there's a windstorm! With all those pillows and blankets, be sure not to fall asleep in there.

here's how...

1. Pretend you're deep in the middle of a forest and you need to build a "fort" to keep you and your playmates safe and dry.

2. Take all the objects you'll need to the couch or largest chair in the house. Challenge yourself to create a deluxe dwelling using the sticks or handles as props for the blanket-walls.

3. The sides should be secured well. Use some shoes to hold the blankets on the ground. Make an opening that closes tightly, so wild animals don't come and bother you.

4. Remember to make a floor that's soft and comfortable. Try pillows with a sheet spread over them. Think about all those imaginary stones and pine needles.

5. Your "building" should be tall enough to stand up in without bending down. You certainly don't want your fort to come crashing down when you jump up because you think you hear a bear outside!

6. You may want a table in your fort for making crafts, reading, or eating.

7. Remember to put everything back that you've borrowed. Be sure everyone gets their sheets and blankets back before bedtime!

How hard

How long

Activity link

Here's a perfect place for *Scary Storytelling* (pages 42–43) or making *Flashlight Monsters* (pages 44–45).

**outdoors
indoors**

nutty noodle people

Your drawings don't always have to be as flat as the paper. You can make them jump off the page with just a little extra effort. Create any type of person, animal, or monster you want! It's easy, and kind of nutty.

Colored construction paper

Pens or pencils

White glue

Nuts with shells

Dried pasta

Buttons, glitter, and other decorations

Popsicle sticks (for variation)

here's how...

1. Take a pen or pencil and draw a person on a piece of construction paper. The figure should be almost as big as the paper. Try to make your drawing as creative as possible. You might want someone silly or someone scary. Use your imagination!

2. Trace the lines you have just drawn with white glue. It should look like you drew the person with the glue.

3. Stick some nuts and noodles onto the white glue. Again, it's time to be creative! Perhaps you'll want to use spaghetti for hair or peanuts for eyes. Maybe you'll want to use macaroni for earrings. That's right—macaroni earrings!

4. You don't have to stop with nuts and noodles. You can add all sorts of things, like buttons, glitter, raisins, and anything else you think your people need to express their unique personalities.

5. See who can make the silliest or the scariest or the most realistic nutty noodle person. The important thing is that the people you create have their own personalities.

6. Make sure to give your people names. Make up stories about them. Where are they from? What special things can they do? What do they do for fun? What do their houses and cars look like? Imagination is the important thing.

...or try this!

You can make your nutty noodle people without drawing them first. Use popsicle sticks for the body and decorate them with noodles and other stuff.

How hard

How long

outdoors
indoors

unfolding stories

Expect the unexpected when your group writes an unfolding story. In this game, both paper and stories unfold together. There will be plenty of giggles and big surprises when you read the twists and turns your story takes.

...or try this!

You can also try this game with pictures instead of words. Just start a drawing and then fold the paper so that only a few lines go over the edge. Have the person next to you add to the artwork and pass it along until there is no more room. Unfold the piece of paper and admire your masterpiece.

here's how...

1. Decide what kind of story you would like to write. Then pick someone to write the opening words. Write the last few words on their own line. Don't give too much away!

2. Fold the paper over so that the next writer can only see the last few words. The person next to you then finishes the sentence in a way that seems to make sense, writes one or two lines of his or her own, and once again folds the paper over to reveal only the last words.

3. Continue to pass the story around until you reach the end of the page. The last writer should think up a dramatic ending.

4. Here's the really fun part. The person who finishes the story gets to unfold the entire piece of paper and read the tale aloud. (Try to get your friends to use their finest handwriting!)

ideas for openings

Spooky: "It was a cold and misty night by the swamp. It was so dark you could hardly see your hands in front of you, and all you could hear was . . ." or "Suddenly, all the lights went out. Tom stood up from the table to try and find a candle, but when he reached inside the kitchen drawer he was shocked to find . . ."

Funny: "Laura noticed that her teacher had a large piece of spinach hanging from her tooth, and to try and forget about it she . . ." or "It wasn't every day you saw a thing like that, at least not as large as the one that sat next to her. The thing didn't seem to mind being stared at, but it did grunt like a . . ."

ideas for endings

Spooky: ". . . and that was the last time the sun set on mysterious Scraggle Swamp." or ". . . and Mike knew that he would never be the same again."

Funny: ". . . and everyone except a squirrel named Gary went totally nuts for acorns." or ". . . and she wiggled her toes like little worms."

How hard

How long

outdoors
indoors

bug dice

Picnics aren't the only places to draw bugs. With this easy-to-play dice game, you can create the scariest—or prettiest—bugs you can imagine. When you're done, your bugs will look so good you'll wish they were alive. Except not on your sandwich.

here's how...

1. Each player rolls one of the dice (a die) in turn. Because the 6 stands for the bug's body, each person has to roll a 6 before beginning to draw. Just keep taking turns rolling the die until a 6 turns up.

2. Each player draws the body of a bug on a sheet of paper with a pen or pencil.

3. Keep taking turns rolling the die, adding different parts onto the body, depending on the numbers you roll. Different numbers match different body parts. You must use all of the numbers at least once!

   6 = body   5 = head   4 = feelers   3 = eyes   2 = legs   1 = tail

4. While you are waiting for a player to roll, keep drawing by putting all sorts of decorations on your bug. But don't add the main parts you have to roll for.

5. Give a big shout when your bug is completed, and call out the name of the kind of bug you drew (it doesn't have to be real). Whoever completes a bug first wins the round. Whoever gets four bugs can be a rock-n-roll band…the Beetles!

How hard

How long

Activity link
Great to play in a *Couch Fort* (pages 34–35).

outdoors indoors

scary storytelling

Every ghost story needs four things—a dark place, a flashlight, a group of people, and a storyteller with imagination. Here are some simple steps for a scary story contest. Whoever faints last is the winner!

here's how...

1. Take a pen or pencil and some paper, and begin to write your scary tale. If you can answer these five questions, you're on your way to making a good story:

   - Who is the story about? One way to scare your listeners and readers is to make them think it might be about them. Make some of the characters seem like your friends.

   - When did it happen? Scary things often happen "on a night just like tonight."

   - Where did it take place? Is there a spooky spot nearby? Creepy swamps, dark tunnels, and abandoned houses are always good choices. Basements and closets can be scary, too.

   - What happened? Fill in the details of the story's plot.

   - Why did it happen? If you can't think of a scary reason for the story's events, it's okay to leave it a mystery.

2. Add specific details. Ask yourself questions like "What color is the haunted bicycle?" and use the answers in your story.

3. Make sure there are twists and turns in the plot that will take your audience by surprise.

4. Read the story out loud to yourself and listen to the way it sounds. Say words like "creak" and "snap" so that they sound like cre-e-e-e-eak and *snap!*

5. Pay extra attention to the ending. It should be the scariest part of the story. One good way to make a story scary is to leave people wondering if it might happen to them. You might want to end by saying something like, "And they say he still rides around the streets in these parts on his haunted bicycle on days just like this."

6. Time to tell your story to whoever dares to listen! Turn off the lights and use a flashlight while telling your story. Or make a fire-less fire circle and think about a man in the forest looking for the tiger that tore off his hand. He walks slowly, very slowly, until he hears a twig snap. Is it on the ground? No! It's in the tree above him. He feels something warm on his neck and . . . BOO!

How hard

How long

Activity link
A *Couch Fort*
(pages 34–35)
makes a great place
to tell scary stories.

**outdoors
indoors**

flashlight monsters

Construction paper

Pens

Scissors and tape

String and popsicle sticks

Sheet (if you need it)

Flashlight

Want to make your own scary monster movies on the wall? You don't need fancy special effects, just a bright flashlight, some dark shadows, and a spooky imagination.

here's how...

1. On construction paper sketch the creatures that you want to star in your movie. Then cut the shapes out. (Simple outlines are easier to cut and project more clearly on your screen.)

2. Make a bunch of different monsters. You might even want to make different versions of the same beast. If you make a lion, a tiger, or a bear, you might want to have one that's running and one that's crouched and ready to pounce. Oh my!

3. Put handles on your monsters. Flying bats look more convincing when they are swooping at the end of a thin piece of string or a pencil than when they are flapping in your hand. A popsicle stick makes a good handle for most nonflying creatures.

4. Find a dark room with a light-colored wall for the show. If there is no light-colored wall, tape up a white sheet to use as the screen. Shine the flashlight on your creations so that they cast their shadows on the screen.

5. See what kinds of special effects you can create: Move the monsters closer and farther away from the light, sweep the light back and forth, shake and wiggle the puppets. Watch how the shadows dance and bend and zoom around.

6. It's time to act out the movie. Have the creatures chase each other back and forth, flying and fighting and just being plain scary. Imagine what their voices would sound like and what they might say. Then add those sounds and voices.

...or try this!

Like the photo shows, you can use your hands to make animal shapes. With a little experimenting, you'll be surprised at the amazing shapes you can produce.

How hard

How long

Activity link

For hints on writing a script to your movie, check out the directions for telling scary stories (pages 42–43).

outdoors
indoors

delicious dirt pies

These dirt pies are much better tasting than s'mores, the ones usually served by the campfire or on the beach. Instead of a shovel, you can use a fork to get every morsel. Be sure to serve with some milk.

Large, resealable plastic bag

Rolling pin

Measuring cups

Small pan

Large bowl and mixing spoon

6 small, disposable bowls

Cookie sheets

Wire racks

Metal bowl and saucepan

Pot holders

here's how...

1. Preheat oven to 350°F.

2. To make the cookie crumbs, peel apart the cookies and scrape out the middle. Put the outside portions inside a resealable plastic bag and seal. Run a rolling pin over the bag until the cookies are crushedinto crumbs.

3. Melt the butter over low heat.

4. Put the melted butter, crumbs, sugar, and salt into a large bowl. Mix well.

5. Press the mixture into the bottom and sides of six small, disposable aluminum bowls.

6. Place the pans on cookie sheets and bake for 10 minutes.

7. Using potholders, take the crusts out of the oven and set aside to cool on wire racks.

8. Now increase the oven temperature to 450°F.

9. Melt the chocolate bars in a metal bowl set over a saucepan of barely simmering water. Keep stirring the chocolate until smooth.

10. Pour the chocolate evenly into the six crusts.

11. Top each pie with marshmallows, pressing them lightly into the chocolate.

12. Put the cookie sheets with the pans of dirt pies into the preheated oven for about 2 minutes, or until the marshmallows are golden.

13. Remove from the oven with pot holders and cool slightly before serving. (That means cool it and wait a few minutes.)

Dirt never tasted so good!

INGREDIENTS

2 cups chocolate cookie crumbs (about 30 cookies), with the cream filling removed

1/4 cup sugar

1/4 teaspoon salt

1 stick (1/2 cup) unsalted butter, melted

6 (about 1 1/2 ounces each) milk chocolate bars

3 1/2 cups mini-marshmallows

How hard

How long

How many
6 servings

outdoors
indoors

star performances

When the sky becomes dark
And the clouds begin storming
Turn on the spotlights
It's time for performing!

Get advice and ideas
Learn to put on a show
You can broadcast the news
Or the worst jokes you know

Make musical instruments
Make puppets from socks
And make cookies to make sure
Your friends don't throw rocks!

star performances

show producer

Old clothes

Old shoes

Old Hats

Makeup

Props

Want to put on a show? Good. Are you excited? Great. Then it's time to get started! There are only three things you need to know to start planning your very own show: What kind will it be? Who's going to come? How many people can you round up to be in it? It's easier than you think. The pages that follow will give you lots of ideas for putting on a star performance!

basic steps for creating a show:

1. Write a script or outline of your show.
2. Give parts to all the players.   3. Design and make costumes and props.   4. Practice the show until it's the way you want it.   5. Invite an audience.
6. Perform your show.   7. Take a bow!

stand-up comedian

Even the funniest people on TV and in the movies started out as kids. And they had to practice their jokes a lot before they became famous. Remember that you can be funny, too, as long as you don't hurt people's feelings. If you have to say something that stings, say it about yourself! And keep laughing.

here's how...

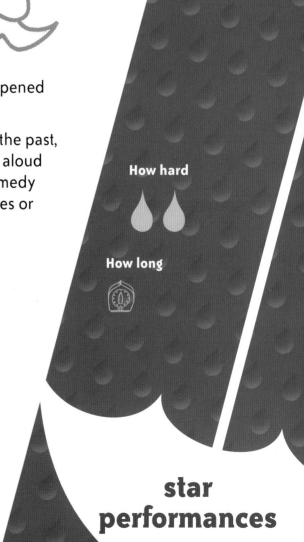

1. The best "bits" (ideas) for your comedy routine usually come from things that have happened in your everyday life. Use examples from family gatherings like holidays, family reunions, or birthday parties. Another good source of ideas is from adventures like going to the zoo or circus, traveling on vacation, or funny things that happened at school.

2. When you think of funny things that have happened in the past, write down little stories about them. You can read them aloud to your audience or ad-lib from them as part of your comedy routine. You should make sure you have at least two jokes or funny parts every minute.

3. The important thing is not to make fun of other people. (That's not funny!) But you can be funny making jokes about yourself.

4. Wear something bright and colorful that shows you are there to have fun. Add other funny costume pieces like funny glasses or a crazy wig—anything to get people in the mood to laugh!

How hard

How long

star performances

song rewriter

There are lots of songs that everyone recognizes the melody to—like "Three Blind Mice" or "Row, Row, Row Your Boat" or "Happy Birthday." You can also change words to songs on TV or radio commercials.

here's how...

1. Use the melody of a song you know, but write your own words. At first, change just a few words. Put in people's names, places, or other things you know. As this gets easier, start changing the words even more.

2. Pass out the words to all of your friends, including the name of the tune you've borrowed.

3. Everyone will instantly be able to sing along, because they know the tune and the beat!

Pen or pencil

Paper

Songbooks

CDs or tapes

Boombox

OPTIONAL ITEMS

Toilet-paper or paper-towel tubes

Tissue paper or newspaper

Tape

lip-synch singer

Most great musicals tell their own story through music.

here's how...

1. Choose a musical that you enjoy, such as *The Lion King, Annie,* or *Beauty and the Beast.* Or pick a tape or CD that you want to pretend you're singing.

2. Listen to the recording a few times to get a feel for the music.

3. Figure out who will sing which parts.

4. Split up the parts and begin to practice.

5. Have everyone get costumes to fit their roles—wigs, masks, or makeup will add lots of fun to the show.

6. Get ready to sing!

...or try this!

To make a microphone, use a toilet-paper or paper-towel tube for the handle. Crumple up tissue paper or newspaper, and tape it to one end for the mike.

How hard

How long

star performances

news reporter

what you need

Poster board

Markers

Tissue paper

Toilet-paper rolls

Everyone tunes in to the local TV newscast to find out the most important things that are going on. Try making your own newscast for your friends, neighbors, and families. You don't need a video camera or a tape recorder to do this. Just imagination. Don't forget to add your own TV commercials.

here's how...

1. Set up a desk that you and a friend can sit behind. The people who read the news are called *anchors* because they hold everything in place.

2. Here are some of the parts other friends can play:

   - **Newscaster.** Who, what, where, when, why? What's going on—in the world, in your city, at your house? You can talk to the audience or interview someone else "on the scene."

   - **Entertainment reporter.** Are there any plays in your community that someone can review? Read any good books lately that can be reported on? How about a review of recent movie releases, videos worth renting, or new television shows?

   - **Sportscaster.** Talk about last weekend's Little League game or sports activities that are going on at school. Talk about your favorite professional teams.

   - **Weather reporter.** Give a summary of the day's weather and what you should be wearing if you are going outdoors.

   - **Special interests reporter.** Report on what's happening that's new or exciting—a bake sale, a school play, a car wash, someone's birthday party, new neighbors. If someone got a new pet, ask her or him to appear on the show.

3. Everyone should take a turn making up commercials. First try to be as serious as possible, then make your next one silly. Bet you can't keep a straight face!

How hard

How long

Activity link
See page 55 for how to make microphones.

star performances

fame game

Did you ever want to be a star? Now's your chance. Get the gang together and take turns playing the lead—the trick is getting your friends to guess which star you are!

58

here's how...

1. Divide your friends into two teams.

2. Give the players three scraps of paper. Everyone should write the name of someone famous on each of the scraps, and fold it so no one else can see. Don't use a name unless at least two people on the other team are likely to identify who it is. The people you name can either be really famous, like movie stars, or just famous to you, like your next-door neighbor who trains parrots to swear. Remember, part of the fun is watching people try to act like the person named.

3. Once everyone has picked a name, each team should put its names in a bowl and hand the bowl to the other team.

4. Everyone can now take turns being a star. One by one, the players pick a name out of their team's bowl and try to get teammates to guess who it is, within 2 minutes. Someone from the other team should watch the clock and call time.

5. To help bring the celebrities to life, try saying something they would say, imitate their voices, act like they would act, or do the things they are best known for. You can also try to describe them in words, but you can't use any part of their name or say any words that sound like their name (no fair saying Barry Groan if you're playing Larry Stone).

6. Every time a team guesses correctly, it should put the paper in a separate pile. If time runs out without getting the right answer, players just announce who they were and toss the name away.

7. No matter whether a team guesses right or not, after each 2-minute turn is up, it is the other team's turn.

8. You can play as long as you want to, but make sure that everyone on both teams gets a chance to be the actor at least once. When the game is over, count up the number of winners each side got. (You might want to give a special People's Choice Award for the actor who gave the wackiest performances.)

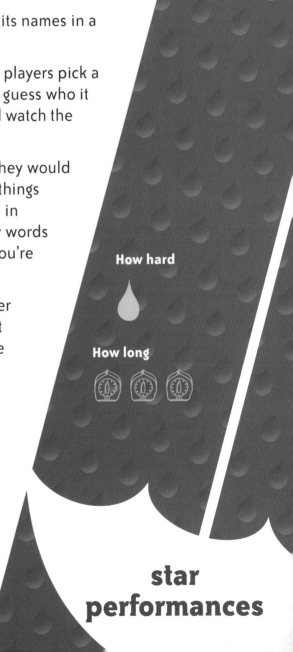

How hard

How long

star performances

puppy puppet maker

Do you know about puppy hand puppets?
If you've got a sock that looks like a pouch
You can make it a pooch in a pinch
Then throw a show with punch!

Tube socks

Pen

Felt or fabric, small pom-poms, premade plastic eyes, ribbon, beads, or other materials like yarn, pipe cleaners, and aluminum foil

Fabric glue or white glue

Scissors

here's how...

1. Lots of socks lose their partners and risk a lonely life in a drawer. You can make a sock happy—find it and put it on one of your hands.

2. Fold your fingers over toward your palm to make an upside-down "L." The puppet's face will go on the back side of your fingers. Now imagine the face of your doggie-to-be.

3. With a pen, mark spots where you want the two eyes to go. You can cut out felt or fabric, or use small pom-poms or premade eyes that you can buy at a crafts store. Anything will do. Attach the eyes with fabric glue or white glue.

4. Using more material, give your puppet a nose. Also attach it with glue.

5. Now cut out a small tongue from red felt or fabric and attach it with glue.

6. Cut out two matching ears and glue them to the sides of the sock. If you are feeling creative, try making ears with spots or other patterns on them.

7. The doggie collar goes where the sock hits your wrists. Use a piece of felt, ribbon, or beads for the collar. Attach with glue.

8. When you've finished using the glue, pull the sock over a used roll of paper towels to dry. This is so the glue won't seep through the middle of the sock and stick both sides together. Let your puppet dry for at least an hour.

...or try this!

Now that you've made a puppy that's as footloose as can be, it's time to make it some friends—other dogs or animals or people. Make a kitty using pipe cleaners for whiskers, or a princess using yarn for long hair and aluminum foil for a crown. Snip two little holes in the sock to pass the whiskers or hair through, and secure with a knot.

How hard

How long

Activity link
Once you've made enough puppets, gather your friends together and put on a show. Turn the page to find out more.

star performances

puppeteer

Put those sock puppets (or other puppets) to work. Follow these simple instructions and you can build your own theater and put on your own puppet show.

what you need

Sofa and room for an audience

or

Table, tablecloth, and chairs

or

2 straight-backed chairs, books, a clothesline, and a blanket or sheet

here's how...

three ways to make a stage

1. You'll need a place to put on your show. If there's room behind the sofa, you can hide back there and ask the audience to sit in front of it on the living room rug or floor.

2. If you have props and scenery you want to use, you'll need a stage with a real floor. The dining room or kitchen table works well—just pull the tablecloth down long enough to hide behind. The audience can sit on the opposite side of the table, where they won't be able to see you.

3. If you want to build a simple puppet theater yourself, take a pair of straight-backed chairs and place them a few feet away from each other. Tie a piece of clothesline between them and set a few heavy books in each chair for balance. Then hang a blanket or sheet from the clothes-line to make a curtain.

and now the show

1. Lights, puppets, action. Send your puppets out on stage and give your show. Remember to use different voices for all the puppets, and move the one who's talking a little bit, so the audience can follow the action.

2. Your show can be as simple or as complex as you want it to be. One or two puppets can sing a song or two, or you can use a crowd of them to tell a long, fanciful story. You can work by yourself behind the stage, or you can use as many other co-puppeteers as will fit behind your stage.

How hard

How long

Activity link
Turn to page 52 for help in putting the ideas for your show together.

star performances

instrument maker

Real music needs real lessons. Pretend music needs pretend instruments and no lessons at all! Learn how to make your own rock-star guitar. Then shake things up with your own maracas (ma-RAK-as)—Spanish-style rattles that keep the rhythm for musicians and dancers.

FOR BOTH

Tempera (poster) paints and brushes

Masking tape

FOR GUITAR, YOU WILL ALSO NEED:

Shoebox

Scissors

4 rubber bands

Stapler or tape

Small stick, pen, or pencil

here's how...

shoebox guitar

1. Using tempera paints and brushes, paint both a shoebox and the box top and let them dry.

2. With the scissors, cut an oval opening in the middle of the shoebox top.

3. Paint a border around the oval opening and let dry.

4. Stretch four rubber bands lengthwise across the top of the box and the oval cutout. If they're not long enough, or if they break, stretch the rubber bands across the opening and use a stapler or tape to hold them in place.

5. Use masking tape to fasten the top and bottom of the box together. Paint the tape if you'd like, but don't get any on your rubber bands!

6. Place a small stick, pen, or pencil under the rubber bands on one side of the box, below where the oval cutout begins.

7. Play "Name that Tune," start a band, or just pluck away!

paper-cup maracas

1. Put a handful or rice or beans in one of the cups.

2. Turn another cup upside down on top of the filled cup. Tape the two cups together, creating a maraca. Repeat this process with the two remaining cups.

3. Mix flour and water together in a mixing bowl to make a thin paste.

4. Tear the newspapers into small strips.

5. Dip the strips into the flour-and-water paste and apply to the maracas in an even layer. Wipe off any excess paste by running the strips through your index finger and thumb.

6. Let the maracas dry overnight.

7. Paint the maracas with bright, loud colors.

8. Shake away!

...or try this!

Fill a plastic bottle with rice or beans and decorate it. No drying needed. Be sure the lid is firmly in place, then shake, rattle, and roll.

How hard

How long

star performances

superstar iced cookies

These cookies are a sure-fire crowd pleaser. Their shape just points out the star that you are. Serve to the other performers and the audience at the cast party after the show!

Large mixing bowl

Electric mixer

Sifter

Medium-sized bowl

Wooden spoon

Star-shaped cookie cutter or table knife

Rolling pin

Cookie sheets

Wire cooling racks

Small mixing bowl

Spoon

Pot holders

INGREDIENTS

COOKIES

1 stick (8 tablespoons) unsalted butter, at room temperature

1 cup sugar

2 cups sifted all-purpose flour

1/4 teaspoon salt

1/2 teaspoon baking powder

1 large egg, lightly beaten

1/2 teaspoon vanilla extract

ICING

1 1/2 cups powdered sugar

1/2 teaspoon vanilla extract

6 tablespoons water

here's how...

making the cookies

1. Put the butter and sugar into a large mixing bowl. Using an electric mixer on low to medium speed, cream them together until the mixture is smooth.

2. Sift together the flour, salt, and baking powder (the dry ingredients) into a medium-sized bowl.

3. Add the dry ingredients to the butter/sugar mixture. Stir with a wooden spoon or with the mixer on low until everything blends together.

4. Add the egg and vanilla, and combine until well mixed.

5. Chill dough in the refrigerator for 1 hour.

6. Preheat oven to 350°F.

7. Lightly flour a rolling pin and a flat area on the kitchen counter.

8. Working carefully, roll the dough $1/8$ inch thick.

9. Cut the dough into star shapes with a cookie cutter or table knife. Then put them on baking sheets, so that they're at least $1/2$ inch apart.

10. Bake the cookies for approximately 10 minutes. Do not let them brown.

11. Using pot holders, remove the baking sheets from the oven and place the cookies on wire racks to cool.

making the icing

1. In a small bowl, use a spoon to blend together the powdered sugar, vanilla extract, and water until the mixture is smooth. Add more water if the icing is too thick to spread.

2. Frost the cookies. Feel free to lick the bowl when you're through. After all, you're the star!

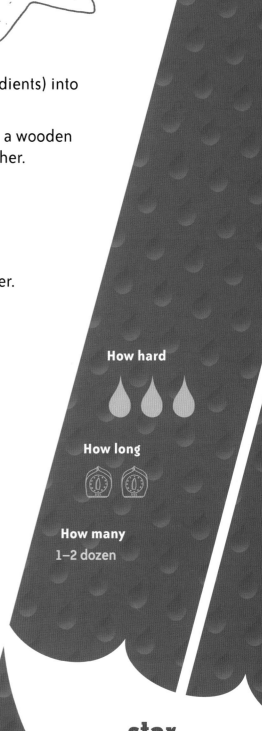

How hard

How long

How many
1–2 dozen

star performances

make helping fun

When the boredom starts flooding
You need a distraction
Wear a cape! Save the world!
Time to jump into action!

Get your bottles and cardboard
Recycle, don't toss 'em
Send your senators letters
It's totally awesome

Make projects for sick kids
Bring a smile when it's pouring
Helping make the world better
Doesn't have to be boring

make helping fun

fantastic hats

what you need

Tape measure

Construction paper

Glitter, feathers, pipe cleaners, aluminum foil, star stickers, or other decorations

Colored cellophane and marking pens

Tape and white glue

Paper clips or clothespins

Is there someone you know—a relative or friend who might be sad or ill—who needs cheering up? Or maybe you're the one who needs to get into a partying mood. Some people say there's nothing that can raise the spirits better than a new hat! The more fantastic, the better.

here's how...

1. Decide whether you want your hat to be part of a costume or just a fabulously crazy hat. Sketch out a design with colored pens on a scrap of paper, and assemble all the materials you'll need to decorate it. You may not have everything you want, so you'll have to make things up as you go along.

2. Using the tape measure, see how big around your head is, just above your ears. (If your hat is for someone else, you can still use your own head as a guide.) Cut a few 2-inch-wide strips of construction paper and tape them together to get one piece that's long enough to go all the way around your head. Use the tape to make the strip into a ring. Test this piece around your head for size. Make sure it's big enough to fit on your head, but not so big that it slips down over your eyes. Set the headband aside.

3. Time to prepare the rest of the hat. If you want to make a space helmet, cut out a half circle and decorate it with stars. Attach pipe cleaner antennae to it, with wads of aluminum foil on the ends to get better deep-space radio reception. If you're making a bird hat, get a bunch of feathers (or draw some and cut them out), and maybe cut out a little bird's head to wear in the front. Draw eyes and a beak on the head. If you want to make a royal crown out of shiny silver, use aluminum foil for the body of the hat and decorate it with colored gems made of construction paper or colored cellophane.

4. Once you've got all of the pieces together, attach them to the headband with white glue and tape. You can use paper clips and clothespins to hold the bigger pieces in place while the glue dries.

5. When the hat is ready, it's time for you—or the person you give the hat to—to get into the mood for getting a-head!

...or try this!

When people want to have a big party, it can't hurt to have special hats on hand. Turn your rainy day into a festival by making fantastic hats like people wear for costume parties, special celebrations, and birthday parties.

How hard

How long

Activity link

It makes sense to wear a colorful mask and a colorful hat at the same time—turn to *Carnaval Mystery Masks* on pages 108–109.

make helping fun

recycling bins

Recycling is the art of reusing and re-creating materials that would have been thrown away and wasted forever. Kids can help the environment simply by recycling the stuff that collects in their home.

74

USUALLY RECYCLABLE

Glass, aluminum, and tin:
- Glass bottles and jars
- Aluminum beverage cans
- Tin food cans
- Aluminum foil and pie tins

Paper and cardboard:
- Newspapers
- Telephone books
- White paper
- Paper bags
- Magazines
- Cardboard from boxes

Plastics:
- Grocery bags (larger)
- Produce bags (smaller)
- Jugs and bottles marked #2 or #4
- Plastic water bottles
- Plastic eating utensils
- Plastic packaging from toys (see if it says it's recyclable)

NOT RECYCLABLE

- Waxed paper
- Waxed milk cartons
- Pet-food bags
- Fast-food wrappers
- Juice boxes
- Pizza boxes
- Stickers

here's how...

1. Get three or more boxes from around your house, or from your local grocery or drug store.

2. Make a label and place it on the front of each box for things you know your community recycles. (Not every community collects the same stuff.) For example, your labels could say NEWSPAPERS, MAGAZINES, PLASTIC, CANS, or PAPER.

3. Decorate the boxes with cutouts from old magazines, photographs, or drawings. Images of nature make great decorations and remind everyone of the benefits of recycling.

4. Place the bins in a good spot and start recycling.

5. From time to time, pack up your recycled goods. If your community picks up recycling, put it out on the right day. Or ask an adult to help you take everything to a local drop-off place.

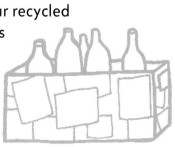

How hard

How long

make helping fun

Construction paper

Colorful pens

Magazines

Scissors

Paper glue or white glue

Poetry book

surprise collage cards

Here's an idea that's both good-hearted and fun: making collage cards. The cards will change depending on who you are making them for. Consider making them for kids or people you don't even know—perhaps get-well cards for sick children who had to go to the hospital, or birthday cards for elderly folks who live in a nursing home or retirement community.

here's how...

doing research

1. Using the Yellow Pages, look up the address and phone number of a local hospital, or find the listing for a nursing or retirement home.

2. Call the hospital to see if it has a children's wing and about how many kids are staying there, or see if a nursing home/retirement home will give you some names of people who have birthdays coming up soon.

making the cards

1. To make two cards, fold an 8½ x 11-inch piece of colored construction paper in half and cut on the crease. Fold and crease each of these pieces in half.

2. Pick some themes for your cards. The sun, kittens, or dogs are a good start.

3. Look through magazines for pictures that fit your themes and cut them out. Also cut out words that are boldly printed in headlines—like Super, Happy, and Fantastic.

5. Arrange your cutouts on the front of your cards until you like the way they look. Add your own artwork using colorful pens.

6. Piece by piece, glue the cutouts to the cards. Be careful not to use too much glue, or the cards will become soggy. Lay the cards out flat to dry.

8. Write some words of get-well cheer or birthday greetings on the card. If you're not sure what to say, look through a book of poetry and copy down the ones that you like the best.

How hard

How long

make helping fun

write a politician

In many countries, every town, city, state, and nation has its own government, filled with politicians who set the rules and make decisions for everyone. If you have suggestions for making changes where you live, write a letter and be heard. You can make a difference!

sample letter

DATE	May 9, 2009
YOUR NAME YOUR STREET ADDRESS YOUR CITY, STATE, ZIP CODE	Alex Raspussen 6655 Elliott Street San Diego, CA 92106
NAME OF OFFICIAL TITLE STREET ADDRESS CITY, STATE, ZIP CODE	Ms. Geraldine Jones Representative of the 16th District 1234 California Way Sacramento, CA 90086
SALUTATION	Dear Representative Jones:
BACKGROUND ABOUT YOU	I am a sixth-grade student at San Diego Elementary School.
THE ISSUE YOU'RE WRITING ABOUT	I am writing to you to let you know that I think our school needs new books. Many of the books in our library are torn and old.
WHAT YOU WANT THE OFFICIAL TO DO	I think you should talk to Congress about giving more money to the public schools.
FINAL REMARKS	Thank you very much for taking the time to read my letter.
CLOSING	Sincerely,
SIGNATURE	*Alex Raspussen*
FULL NAME	Alex Raspussen

here's how...

doing research

It's important to find the *right* person to write to about something you are concerned about. This may take some sleuthing. The easiest place to start is in the Blue Pages of your telephone book. To find a local official, check under the name of your city or county. If it's a state issue, find the name of your representative to the legislature. For national problems, write to one of the U.S. senators representing your state.

writing your suggestion

1. You'll probably want to draft your letter first using scratch paper and pencil, then pen the final version onto a piece of stationery.

2. The sample letter shown here gives the parts of a letter and where they go. But the most important part of writing a letter is the subject. Always write about things you really care about. If you have ideas about what the government should do to solve the problem, say so.

3. Write your name, address, city, state, and ZIP code on the top left-hand corner of the envelope. Put the name, address, city, state, and ZIP code of the person you are writing to in the middle of the envelope. Put a postage stamp in the upper right-hand corner. When the letter is safely inside and the enveloped sealed, it's time to mail it.

4. Don't be too surprised if you receive a letter back from the official—mailed just to you—telling you how glad she or he was to hear from you!

How hard

How long

make helping fun

continuous calender

Measuring tape and calculator

Ball of string, scissors, and pencil

3–4 colors of poster board

3–4 felt-tipped markers of matching colors

365 round tags (1³/₄ inches in diameter) and string loops

Clothespins

Tape and tacks

Watch time marching around a room or hallway by making a calender that never ends. This is a good way to keep track of special occasions as they relate to the past, present, and future. It's not only a visual tool for learning about time and counting, but also a fun way for the whole family to be aware of upcoming events.

here's how...

1. Find some long, continuous space in a room your family uses all the time, like a kitchen, family room, or hallway. For the calendar to be continuous, figure going across, over, or under any windows or doors that are in the way. For 365 tags, 1 3/4 inches in diameter and spaced 1 inch apart, you'll need about 1,000 inches, or 83 feet! So for a room with four 10-foot-wide walls, you'll have to go around the room twice. Measure the space and then do a little math to calculate how much space you can put between each tag.

2. Cut pieces of string for each path the calendar will take. Allow a couple of inches at each end for taping or tacking to the wall. Then put your string in place. Make sure to get permission first.

3. Decide which color to use for each month. Using colored marking pens, number the tags on both sides from 1 to 30 or 31, depending on the month.

4. Tie the numbered tags for each month onto the sections of string, then securely attach the string onto the wall using tacks and tape—whatever works best. Try to space the tags evenly; the different colors tell when a new month begins.

5. Cut out strips of poster board to match the colors of the numbers, and write the names of the months on them. Put them above the 30 or 31 numbers representing that month.

6. To mark Yesterday, Today, and Tomorrow, make signs and tape them to clothespin handles. Clamp the clothespins to the appropriate date tags, and move them forward every day. To mark special events, hang pictures or labels from clothespins and attach them to the day tags—a birthday hat and someone's name, a jack-o'-lantern, a Star of David, a Christmas tree, for example.

...or try this!

At leap year every four years, add one more tag for February 29th. Or always include a tag for that date, and three out of four years explain why you have to skip that day!

How hard

How long

make helping fun

bowwow biscuits

The doggies at your local animal shelter will howl with delight when they eat these easy-to-make treats! (Check with the shelter first to see if dogs can accept homemade food.) Also share these biscuits with the dogs in the neighborhood. This is called dog-unity service.

Measuring cups

Large mixing bowl

Large wooden spoon

Electric mixer

Waxed paper

Rolling pin

Baking sheets

Knife or cookie cutter

Airtight container

82

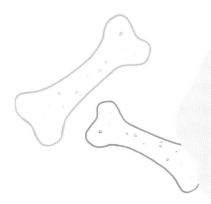

INGREDIENTS

2 cups whole-wheat flour

1 1/2 cups quick-cooking oats, uncooked

1/4 cup wheat germ

1/4 cup cornmeal

1/2 cup vegetable oil

1/4 cup chicken or beef broth

1/2 cup peanut butter, chunky or creamy

1/4 cup honey

1 egg

here's how...

1. Preheat the oven to 350°F.

2. Measure out all ingredients and put them into a large mixing bowl.

3. Mix everything together using a large wooden spoon. Or use an electric mixer on medium speed. Keep going until the ingredients are completely moistened.

4. Make a ball out of half the dough and put it onto a large sheet of waxed paper.

5. Cover the dough with another piece of waxed paper, then roll the dough until it is about 1/4 inch thick. Remove the top piece of waxed paper.

6. Using a knife, cut the dough into small 1-inch squares. Repeat this process with the other half of the dough. If you happen to have a cookie cutter shaped like a dog bone, use it instead of the knife. Or pick cookie-cutter shapes you think a doggie would enjoy. (Hint: They like delivery people.)

7. Remove the biscuits from the waxed paper and place them slightly apart on two ungreased baking sheets.

8. Place the cookie sheets in the oven on the top and middle racks and bake for 15 minutes.

9. Turn off the oven. Leave the biscuits in the oven to dry for 2 hours.

10. When you take the dog biscuits out of the oven, put them into an airtight jar or tin. Now round up a dog or two and see if they drool over them! Fight the urge to sink your teeth into them yourself.

How hard

How long

How many
4 dozen

make helping fun

sunshine cupcakes

These yellow cupcakes are topped with a sweet cream-cheese icing that will please every sweet tooth. For an extra jolt of colorful sugar, add your favorite sprinkles. Great for passing out to your neighbors, family, and friends.

12-hole muffin tin

Muffin-tin liners

Measuring cups

Measuring spoons

Sifter

Medium- and large-sized bowls

Electric mixer

Liquid measuring cup

Large spoon

Wooden skewer

Flat knife

Pot holders

INGREDIENTS

CUPCAKES

2 cups sifted pastry flour

2 teaspoons baking powder

Pinch of salt

1 stick unsalted butter, at room temperature

3/4 cup sugar

2 eggs

1 teaspoon vanilla extract

3/4 cup milk, at room temperature

ICING

1 can premade cream-cheese icing

Sprinkles (if you want them)

here's how...

making the cupcakes

1. Preheat the oven to 350°F.

2. Line a 12-hole muffin tin
   (or two 6-hole tins) with paper liners.

3. Measure the flour, baking powder, and salt
   into the sifter. Sift it all into a medium-sized bowl. Set aside.

4. Put the butter into a large bowl. Using an electric mixer on medium speed,
   cream the butter until soft.

5. Add the sugar to the creamed butter, and beat with the electric mixer
   until the mixture is light and fluffy.

6. Add the egg yolks and continue beating until they are mixed in. Add the
   vanilla at the end.

7. Add the flour mixture and the milk to the creamy mixture in parts like
   this: flour, milk, flour, milk, flour. Using the electric mixer's low setting
   or a large spoon, stir the batter until smooth.

8. Using a large spoon, divide the batter evenly into the lined
   muffin-tin holes.

9. The cupcakes should bake for 20 minutes. Test them with a
   wooden skewer or butter knife. When it comes out clean (not
   sticky) when poked into the middle of a cupcake, the cupcakes
   are ready.

10. Carefully take the tin out of the oven using pot holders. Let
    the cupcakes cool completely before adding the icing.

icing the cupcakes

1. Divide the icing evenly among the 12 cupcakes and
   smear it on with a knife.

2. Add sprinkles on top, if desired, and arrange on a plate.
   Now dig in!

How hard

How long

How many
1 dozen

**make
helping fun**

color away the gray

When the rain's on your brain
And the day can't be duller
You can say there's a way
You can add some more color

Make real magic wands
And Bam! go the blues
Wild animal critters
Appear out of shoes

First make a crazy picture
Then make a crazy frame
Go bananas with a smoothie
Your kitchen won't be the same!

color away the gray

fancy frames

What's the best way to frame your friends and family? This frame is more than bright—it's brilliant art. Make it as a gift, for yourself or for someone else. Decorate with shells, buttons, pebbles, or even dried cereal and pasta. Picture that!

Picture frame, made either from wood or heavy cardboard

White glue and plastic knife

Assorted beads, sequins, feathers, pom-poms, and other small decorations

Cutouts from magazines

here's how...

1. Cover a work surface with newspapers so the glue doesn't get everywhere.

2. Lay a store-bought frame down flat.

3. Apply an even layer of glue at one corner of the frame. Use a plastic knife to make the glue even, if you need to.

4. Add the beads one by one, pressing each one firmly into the glue. When you are finished with one corner, let the frame dry for 15 minutes.

5. Begin steps 1 to 4 at the next corner, and repeat until all four corners are finished.

6. Fill in the rest of the frame with glue and beads.

7. Let the frame dry for a few hours.

8. Now fill the frame with a photograph or drawing.

9. Warning: Sometimes the frame looks better than the picture!

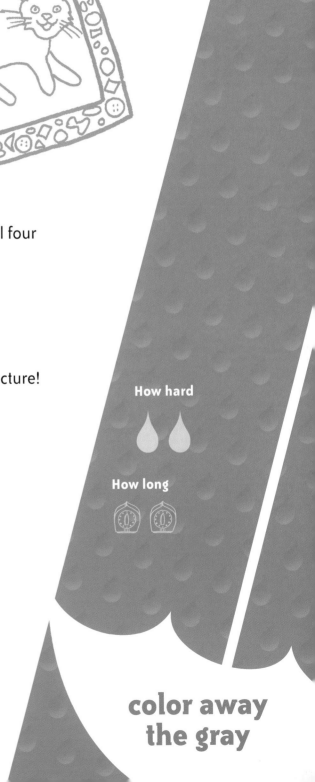

How hard

How long

color away the gray

sole mates

Here's a creative way to recycle those old shoes. Just make sure you don't use your mom's favorite footwear. (Hint: Get permission.) In no time, you'll have your own "sole" mate.

here's how...

1. Pick any shoe that's ready to be thrown away—size, shape, and color don't matter. You can keep any laces as part of your design, or take them out. The design can be anything your imagination dreams up, such as an animal, an alien, a person, a car, a ship, a spaceship, or an original pattern, to name only a few possibilities.

2. Using a variety of objects, start creating by gluing stuff to the shoe. You might want to try beads, buttons, goggly eyes (the ones that are used in crafts and on stuffed animals), yarn, pipe cleaners, feathers, pom-poms, fabric, fake fur, ping-pong balls, you name it.

3. What to do with it? Use it for a paper weight? Create its twin? You might even want to wear it!

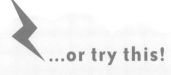

...or try this!

Make your sole mate right at home (or left at home if it's a left shoe). Decorate a shoebox to match the style of your sole mate. Home is where the art is!

How hard

How long

color away the gray

attractive magnet frames

Lots of people use magnets on their refrigerators for artwork, school papers, photographs, and grocery lists. Why not make this special magnet frame that is a work of art in itself? Use it to hang little drawings or collages you've made, photos of your parents, or anything else that fits in its window. You can custom-make a few frames for your favorite pictures.

White paper

Ruler

Scissors

White glue

Magnetized tape, 1/2 inch wide

Paints and marking pens

Aluminum foil (an option)

94

here's how...

1. Your frame can be any size, but these instructions are for a 5 x 7-inch frame that will hold art or photos up to 4 x 6 inches in size. Cut a 5 x 7-inch rectangle out of a piece of white paper.

2. Flip the paper upside down and draw a line down each side, 1 inch in from the edge. That will be the edge of the inside of the frame. It's also the line on which you will line up your magnets.

3. Curl the paper over in half, without making a crease. With the scissors nip a tiny cut out of the middle. From this hole start cutting toward the edge of the paper. Cut out the inside of the frame along the lines you drew in step 2 until you've cut out all four sides and made a hole for your artwork or photo.

4. Turn the page right-side up again. It's time to decorate your frame. Draw or color on the paper to make a decorative design.

6. Cut four ¹/₂-inch strips of magnetized tape: two 5 inches long and two 6 inches long. If you don't have any tape, just cut ¹/₂-inch strips of a flexible, business-card-sized magnet until you get the right lengths. Peel off the adhesive backing on the tape and stick it to the inside edge of the back of your frame. Or glue the magnet strips down.

7. Make signs and announce your own art show.

...or try this!

You can use aluminum foil to give your frame a modern metallic look. Cut a piece of foil that's about 1 inch wider than the frame (for a 5 x 7-inch frame, that would be about 6 x 8 inches). Fold the edges of the foil over the outside of the frame and glue them down. Use the technique described in step 3 to cut the foil. When it is trimmed, fold the inside flap to the back of the frame and glue it down, too.

How hard

How long

color away the gray

concentration cards

Some experts say it's hard for a brain to concentrate when it's rainy. But what do they know? Maybe they're experts at fixing refrigerators, not brains. Find out for yourself. Make your own colorful deck of cards for playing the game Concentration.

...or try this!

Draw all the matching pictures yourself on index cards. Or you and another person can draw the same thing—a horse, a car, someone you know—then try to match them when you play!

here's how...

making the cards

1. Flip through some magazines and find pictures that you like.

2. Find pairs of pictures with matching colors. You can either use half of the same piece of blue sky or find two pictures that have the same color in them—perhaps a sports team uniform, green grass, or white snow. You can also cut a picture of something in half, so that together they make a "match." Or find two pictures that go together for other reasons.

3. Cut out (or separate) pictures, and glue them to index cards.

4. Make as many pairs as you wish. The more pairs you make, the more challenging the game will be. Just make sure you don't make more than can fit on your floor or table at the same time.

playing the game

1. Turn the cards over and shuffle them to mix up the pairs. Now lay them out on the floor or table, facedown.

2. Time to play! Everyone takes turns flipping over two cards, trying to make a match. If the cards you turn over make a pair, pile them up in front of yourself and take another turn. If you don't make a match, flip the cards back over, facedown, and leave them where they were. Let the next person take a turn.

3. Pay attention during other players' turns and try to remember where certain colored cards are, so it will be easier for you to make a match when it's your turn.

4. When all the cards are matched, count the piles and see who's got the most.

How hard

How long

Activity link
A great place to play Concentration is in a *Couch Fort* (pages 34–35).

color away the gray

presto! magic wands

One of the best ways to make a wish come true is to use a magic wand! Wave the wand in the air and say your wishes out loud. You can also use the wand for granting make-believe wishes to your friends. The dangling ribbons or pieces of fabric are colorful and dance through the air.

here's how...

1. Use the stick or dowel as the handle for the wand. One end will be for holding, and the other end will be decorated with the ribbons.

2. Make sure you have 10 strips of ribbon or fabric, about 6 inches long and about an inch wide.

3. Lay the wand down on newspapers or a work surface that glue won't ruin.

4. Smear a small amount of glue on one end of the ribbon, and attach the glue side of the ribbon to the top of the wand.

5. Continue gluing all the pieces of the ribbon around the top of the wand. Make sure you place the ribbon at the same point on the stick, all the way around, so that you have an even edge.

6. Let the wand sit for 20 minutes, or until it's dry.

7. Turn the wand upside down, so that the streamers are hanging away from the stick.

8. Smear glue all over the 2-inch piece of ribbon or fabric and wrap it around the top of the wand. This creates a border on top of where the other ribbons are glued.

9. Let the wand dry for 20 minutes.

10. Turn the wand back upright and the ribbons will fall back over the wand like a waterfall.

11. Glue decorations onto the ribbon or fabric that will glitter or move when you turn the wand.

12. Make a wish!

How hard

How long

Activity link
Magic wands go great with *Fantastic Hats* (pages 72–73).

color away the gray

shapely beanbags

Strong piece of fabric, like felt

Magic marker

Scissors

Needle and thread, fabric glue, or stapler

Dried beans or uncooked rice

Decorations, fabric glue, and felt-tipped pens

A beanbag in a shape is a fun way to throw food around the house—without getting into trouble or making a mess. It's easy to sew a fabric pouch, fill it with beans, and send your creation flying in a game of catch.

here's how...

making the beanbag

1. Find some fabric and fold it in half. Be sure to pick something fairly thick, so that the insides don't escape all over the floor.

2. Draw a simple shape on the fabric with a magic marker.

3. Cut out your shape, keeping the fabric folded in two, so that you end up with a front and a back half.

4. Sew, glue, or staple the two pieces of material together around the edges, leaving a hole big enough for the stuffing. When you're finished, turn it inside out.

5. Fill your shape with uncooked rice or beans. Don't pack it too tightly or it could burst when you throw it!

6. Sew up or staple the hole.

7. Depending on its size, your beany shape will also make a good paperweight or hanging ornament.

decorating the beanbag

To add some life to your beanbag creation, put some glue on the finished shape and attach some of the leftover rice or beans. You can also stick on some glitter or little bits of colored wool. Felt-tipped pens make it easy to add details to your shape, like a crawly caterpillar on a leaf. But make sure it can take lots of throwing!

How hard

How long

color away the gray

smushy smoothies

What would you get if a fruit truck, an ice truck, a dairy truck, and a beekeeper's truck all crashed into each other? A street full of smoothies—and bees. Be sure to look both ways before scooping some up.

INGREDIENTS

ISLAND SMOOTHIE

1 1/2 cups unsweetened pineapple juice

8 slices pineapple   1 banana

4 teaspoons sugar   Ice cubes

BANANA SURPRISE

3 cups milk   4 ripe bananas

1/2 teaspoon vanilla   Ice cubes

2 teaspoons honey

BANANA SPLIT

1 cup chocolate milk   2 frozen bananas

RED ROOSTER

2 cups raspberries

2 cups orange juice

1/4 cup honey

1/2 cup plain yogurt

Ice cubes

MOOLESS MANGO

2 cups vanilla soy milk

2 cups frozen mango chunks

1 banana

here's how...

1. To freeze fruit, like the bananas or mangos in these smoothie recipes, peel and break the bananas in half or cut mangos into chunks. Place the fruit in resealable plastic bags and freeze.

2. To make any of the smoothies, put all the ingredients in a blender and blend until smooth and creamy.

3. Serve in frosted glasses (put them in the freezer until frost forms on them—not too long or they'll crack).

4. Pretend your smoothie is really junk food... and enjoy!

How hard

How long

How many
2–4 glasses

**color away
the gray**

around the world

Why stay home today
Watching TV like goats?
You can travel the world
Without raincoats or boats

Fold your own butterfly
Try crafts even older
Like Spanish mosaics
Or a pioneer's pot holder

Tell stories in beads
With an African necklace
Fun to make them and wear them
(Except if you're neckless!)

around the world

carnaval mystery masks

Carnaval (car-na-VAL) is a holiday that's celebrated in many places as the last time to have lots of fun before Lent. One city that's famous for its costumes, dancing, music, and parades is Rio de Janiero, Brazil. In the United States, the heart of the celebration is New Orleans, Louisiana. During Carnaval, people wear all kinds of masks, which adds to the fun. So make your own mask and get into a partying mood.

Poster board

Scissors

Pencil

Tempera (poster) paints and brushes

Decorations such as sequins, beads, feathers, shells

Hole punch

2 feet (24 inches) of thin ribbon

here's how...

1. Make a working surface on a table by spreading out newspapers or paper towels that you can throw away later.

2. On poster board, use a pencil to trace the shape of a mask. Be creative. The mask can be any shape, but should cover your eyes and fit above your nose. Cut out the mask with scissors.

3. Place the mask up to your face to test for size. The two ends should touch each side of your face just before the ears. Adjust the size of the mask if it is too big.

4. Have a friend mark lightly on the mask with a pencil where the holes for your eyes need to be.

5. Put your mask back on the table. Cut out the eye holes, using a decorative shape. Hold the mask up to your face again to make sure you can see out of the eye holes. Keep cutting until you can see through the holes.

6. Paint the mask using a washable, nontoxic paint. Make it zany and colorful.

7. Allow the paint to dry about 20 minutes.

8. Decorate the mask with any materials you have on hand: feathers and sequins look great; so do beads, seashells, and extra paint.

9. Using a hole punch, make a hole at each end of the mask where it meets an ear.

10. Cut two pieces of ribbon, each 1 foot (12 inches) long.

11. Thread the ribbons through the holes and tie them with a knot.

12. Tie the ribbons around the back of your head to hold the mask on your face.

13. Now you can pretend to be anyone or anything in your mask. Time to party on down!

How hard

How long

Activity link
Masks can be worn on lots of festive occasions, along with *Fantastic Hats* (pages 72–73).

around the world

spanish paper mosaics

In the ancient world, artists used tiny bits of colored stone and ceramic to make durable works of art in floors and walls. Some of the most attractive ancient mosaics appear in Spain, influenced by the Roman and Islamic mosaic traditions. Now it's time to make a mosaic influenced by YOU!

Sketching paper or graph paper

Colored construction paper

Scissors

Hole punch (optional)

White glue

Chopsticks, popsicle sticks, or toothpicks

Ruler or straight edge

110

here's how...

1. Decide what kind of mosaic you want to make. Realistic? Simple? Abstract? Geometric (lines, circles, and other shapes)? You can copy interesting patterns from a piece of fabric that you like or from natural forms like leaves or waves on the ocean.

2. Sketch your design on a piece of blank paper. If you want to be really accurate, you can use graph paper.

3. Cut out the pieces of colored paper you will need for your design. Cut out large pieces with scissors. If you want lots of perfect little circles, use a hole punch. If you want to make a mosaic quickly, try a simple pattern with big chunks of color. If you have the patience to go all day, make a complex design with tiny pieces.

4. Select a piece of construction paper for your background. Choose a color that isn't too close to any of the colors in your pattern, so that the design will stand out from the background. Black works well.

5. Squeeze out a tiny dab of glue onto the end of one of the chopsticks (if chopsticks aren't handy, use a popsicle stick or a toothpick), and put the glue on the spot where you want your first colored piece to go. Position the colored speck on the glue, and then tamp it in place with the clean end of the other chopstick, popsicle stick, or toothpick.

6. Repeat step 5 until you have finished your mosaic. Make sure that all the pieces go just where you want them. Once they're glued down, they're stuck—and so are you. To make sure nothing will fall off, carefully move a ruler or other straight edge over your mosaic, then add more glue as needed.

...or try this!

Try ripping instead of cutting to give your mosaic pieces interesting edges. You might also want to use the paper that you've punched holes out of, letting the background color show through.

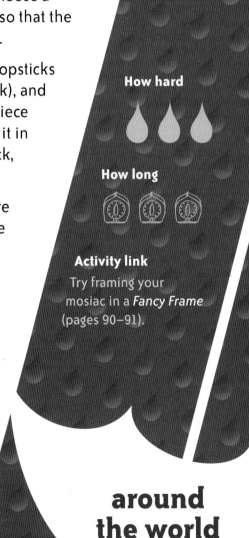

How hard

How long

Activity link
Try framing your mosiac in a *Fancy Frame* (pages 90–91).

around the world

african bead necklaces

For thousands of years people have worn beads. In Africa, beads were also used instead of money for trading and have many other cultural meanings, based on color and pattern. The Zulu can tell a lot about people they meet just by looking at their necklaces and reading the story that is written in the beads. Let's see what your bead necklace says about you!

Towel

Variety of beads with large holes

3 yards (9 feet) of kite string

Scissors

White glue (or beading needle)

Tape

here's how...

1. Set a towel out on your working surface to keep the beads from rolling away.

2. Choose the beads you want to use and decide on a pattern. Do you want to alternate colors and sizes? Do you want to stick to a carefully designed pattern or let your necklace go a little wild? Lay the beads into the design you want or into piles of certain types and colors. Set aside about a dozen extra-special beads for the center of the necklace, where they will be the most visible.

3. Cut three strands of kite string, each 1 yard (3 feet) long. Tape one end of each string to the table or surface you are working on, and stiffen each of the other ends with little dabs of glue. When the glue dries, the strands will be much easier to push through the holes in the beads. You can use a beading needle instead of the tape-and-glue method.

4. String 10 inches of beads on each separate strand.

5. Next, connect all three strands and pass them through one of the special centerpiece beads. Then separate the three strands and pass each through a single smaller bead. Repeat until you've used up your special beads.

6. Now thread the second side of the necklace, just like you did the first side: Separate the strings and put 10 inches of beads on each single strand.

7. Untape the strings from the table and put all six ends of the string together. Feed them through two medium-sized beads.

8. Leave 2 inches of plain string at the ends of each strand, then tie the necklace off with an overhand knot. Leaving a few inches of fringe, trim the extra string with scissors.

How hard

How long

around the world

pioneer pot holders

Cardboard
(from box or
writing tablet)

Scissors

Ruler and pen

Scraps of cotton
cloth

Large safety pin

Popsicle stick

When Europeans first came to North America in the 1600s, settling in what became Canada and the United States, they had to make almost everything they used themselves. For instance, they wove their pot holders on homemade wooden looms. Here's how you can make a loom and weave a pot holder yourself.

here's how...

making the loom

1. To make a loom, you'll need a piece of sturdy cardboard, like the back of a pad of writing paper or a piece of a cereal box or shoe box.

2. Cut the cardboard into a 7-inch square. Using a ruler, mark lines every 1/4 inch along the top and bottom of the cardboard. At each line, cut out a notch about 1/4 inch deep. When you're done, the notches should look like rows of sawteeth.

making the pot holder

1. Cut scraps of cloth into strips about 1/4 inch wide. Use old T-shirts, blue jeans, towels, or any other kind of cotton cloth. It can be all one color and kind of cloth, or all the colors of the rainbow with lots of different textures, depending on how you want your pot holder to look.

2. String strips of the cloth back and forth through the notches on the top and bottom of the loom. These vertical strands of material are called the *warp*. When you get to the end of a strip, tie it onto the next one using a double knot, and keep going.

3. Now you can start weaving. Attach a strip of cloth to a large safety pin and run it across the loom, up and over one strand of the warp, and then down and under the next. You are making the *weft*.

4. When you reach the end of the row, turn around and go back. This time, go over all the warp you went under and under all the ones you went over. Don't pull too tight when you turn around at the end of the row, or the pot holder won't stay square. Use the popsicle stick to pack all the rows snug and tight against the rows that are on top of them.

5. When you get to the end of a strip, start the new one back a few inches so that the weaves overlap a little bit.

6. When you have woven all the way to the bottom of the loom and have packed the rows in as tightly as you can, bend the cardboard back so you can pop the pot holder off of the loom. Smooth out the rows with your fingers so that they are even and fill out the loops of the warp.

How hard

How long

Activity link
Use one or two of your own handsome, handmade pot holders to cook the recipes in this book.

around the world

mexican piñata

Piñatas are fun to make, but can take a few days to complete. A piñata is a pottery or paper container, brightly decorated and filled with candy and sometimes toys. On holidays and at parties, each child is blindfolded and tries to break the piñata by hitting it with a stick or bat. When the piñata breaks, candy falls everywhere! The child who breaks it is the hero/heroine of the festival, and the candy is shared by all.

Large balloon

Mixing bowl

Flour and water

Newspapers

Tempera (poster) paints and brushes

Scissors and string

Candy

Broomstick or pole

Scarves or cloth napkins

here's how...

1. Blow up the balloon, but not too tightly.

2. Put a little flour in a mixing bowl, and add just enough water to make a thin paste.

3. Tear the newspapers into strips that are 1 1/2 inches wide and 5 inches long.

4. Dip the newspaper strips into the flour-and-water paste and apply them to the balloon. Wipe off any excess paste by running the strips between your index finger and thumb.

5. Place the strips on the balloon at an angle and slightly overlap them. Continue adding the strips to the balloon until the entire balloon is covered, except for a 2-inch square at the top. Let the strips dry for a few hours.

6. When the piñata is dry, go wild painting your piñata with bright, festive colors. It is easier to paint the piñata with the balloon still inside.

7. After the paint has completely dried, pop the balloon and push the candy through the top hole.

8. Poke small holes on opposite sides of the top square hole. Put string through the small holes and secure them by making knots at the bottom.

9. Tie the piñata onto a broomstick or pole. Blindfold your friends and have them try to knock the piñata open with a shorter stick.

10. Someone can hold the stick with the piñata and move it away from the blindfolded person who is swinging. This makes the game last longer. Be sure to stay out of the way!

11. After everyone has had a few turns, it should get easier to hit the piñata. Remember: When it opens, everyone shares the loot!

...or try this!

You can stretch this activity out for an entire rainy week, if you like. Simply keep pasting on more newspaper strips as soon as a layer is dry. This will make the piñata harder to break!

How hard

How long

Activity link
Serve *Sunshine Cupcakes* (pages 84–85) at your next piñata party.

around the world

japanese origami butterflies

Origami paper
or wrapping
paper or
colored paper

Plastic pen or
hard-edged
object

Origami (OR-i-GA-mi) is the traditional Japanese art of paper sculpture. Although it's possible to make useful items like boxes and paper cups, most origami forms are made for ceremonial and decorative uses. When making origami, read all the steps first, so you'll put folds in the right places.

here's how...

1. Start with a rectangle of paper that's twice as wide as it is high. Or make a square and cut it in half. If you have origami paper or wrapping paper, start with the colored side up. Make a crease down the middle and then unfold it. The crease will tell you where the center of the paper is. Hint: Make your first folds carefully. Once you're sure a fold is in the right spot, make a final crease with your fingernail, or the edge of a plastic pen, or something with a hard edge.

2. Fold corners A and B behind, so that they meet at the center. This kind of fold is called a *mountain fold*, because the crease is like the peak of a mountain.

3. Fold lines EC and ED up and in, so that they meet at the center crease. Let corners A and B pop back up.

4. Turn the paper over and make a *valley fold* (the crease is like the center of the valley) down the middle, this time horizontally, from B to A. Now valley-fold side E down to the center, and then straighten it back up.

5. Refold the creases from the last step, but this time, tuck corner E up and under the horizontal flap at the bottom.

6. Making vertical creases, mountain-fold the loose corners behind as far as they can go. You're trying to tuck back the upper layer of the wing so the layer underneath can peek out.

7. Form the body of the butterfly by making a mountain fold and two valley folds. This should help swivel the wings apart at corners D and C.

8. Your finished butterfly can take wing. Beautiful!

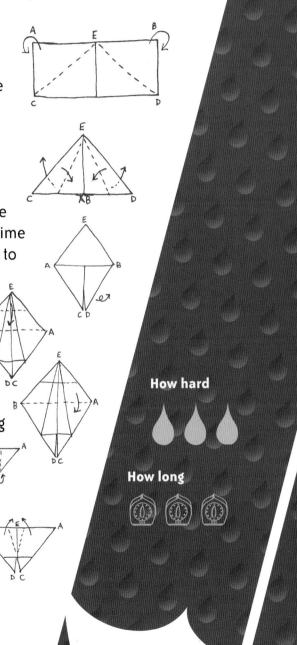

How hard

How long

around the world

what you need

native american button blankets

Button blankets were created by the Native Americans of the Pacific Northwest coast region. When European traders brought manufactured blankets and buttons to the area, the native artists adapted them to their traditional art forms in beautiful new designs.

here's how...

1. A button blanket is cloth that has been decorated with a design made of buttons. Traditional button blanket designs often had special meaning for their wearers, reflecting important events in their or their family's lives or histories. Think of a design that means something special to you. Sketch your design on a piece of scratch paper. Use multicolored pens to indicate the different colors of buttons you want to use.

2. To make a simple blanket, outline the shape of the figures in your design with buttons. For a more intricate blanket, fill in the colors with solid fields of buttons. You can even button-color the whole background. The number of buttons you have and how much time you want to spend will help you decide how dense you want your blanket to be.

3. With scissors, cut a piece of thread that stretches to your elbow. Thread a needle, even out the strands on either side of the needle's eye, and tie a knot through the ends.

4. When you're ready to start sewing, make a few stitches through the blanket in the spot where you want the first button to go. Put a button over the stitches, and then sew through each of the holes of the button a few times so it won't fall off. When you run out of thread, tie off the strands.

5. Line up the buttons so the holes all face the same way, and use the same pattern for sewing all your buttons (making an "X" or a square through the button holes). Or do a different pattern for different kinds and colors of buttons.

6. The thread connecting the buttons and the starting and ending knots can look pretty messy. This work should be on the reverse side of your blanket—it's not for show!

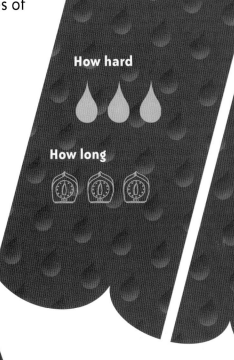

How hard

How long

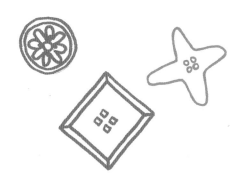

around the world

italian pizza buns

These buns are made like sticky morning buns but without all the sweet stuff. They are perfect, palm-sized, snack-a-licious pastries!

- 12-hole muffin tin
- Muffin-tin paper liners
- Large cutting board
- Rolling pin
- Measuring spoons
- Measuring cups
- Spreading knife
- Cheese grater
- Large cutting knife
- Pot holders

INGREDIENTS

1 package (10 ounces) premade pizza crust dough

A little flour

6 tablespoons favorite pizza sauce

1 cup mozzarella cheese

1/4 cup grated Parmesan cheese

here's how...

1. Preheat oven to 400°F.

2. Line a 12-hole muffin tin (or two 6-hole tins) with paper liners.

3. Take the pizza crust dough out of the refrigerator or freezer. After the dough is soft (at room temperature), place it onto a large, lightly floured cutting board (or a surface you can cut on). Using the rolling pin, roll out the dough into a rectangle that measures about 12 x 8 inches.

4. Spread the pizza sauce evenly over the dough, leaving a small border of dough around the edges.

5. Sprinkle the mozzarella cheese evenly over the sauce.

6. Starting with the long side, roll the dough into a tight log, like rolling up a carpet. Place the end of the roll facedown on the table.

7. Cut the log into 12 equal slices.

8. Place the pieces, cut side up, into the lined muffin-tin holes.

9. Sprinkle the top of each bun with Parmesan cheese.

10. Bake for 10 minutes or until golden brown.

11. Using pot holders, remove the buns from the oven and allow to cool slightly before serving.

12. As they say in Italy, "Mangia (eat)!"

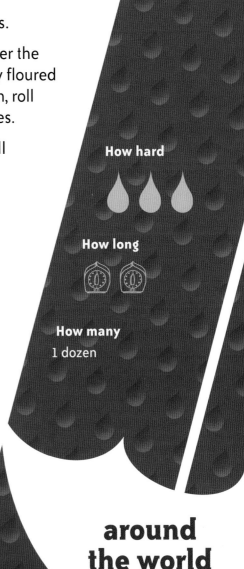

How hard

How long

How many
1 dozen

around the world

index

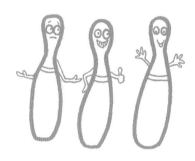

Orange Avenue creates a wide variety of books for young readers.

Its creative partners, Hallie Warshaw and Mark Shulman, believe that the best children's books excite their readers' imaginations, encouraging them to think and learn.

Orange Avenue is based in San Francisco and New York. For information about Orange Avenue and its products, go to www.orangeavenue.com.

Hallie Warshaw loves children's books and bright colors.

Before founding Orange Avenue, Inc., Hallie was a creative director for a large educational publisher. She has also been a graphic designer and art director in Hong Kong, Osaka, and New York. Without a doubt, however, the most influential experience in creating this book was being an arts-and-crafts counselor at Lake Farm summer camp in Cape Cod.

Hallie holds bachelor degrees from Clark University in Worcester, Massachusetts, and the Rhode Island School of Design in Providence.

She lives in San Francisco in a pastel blue building that she wishes was painted bright orange.

Mark Shulman writes for children and adults.

He was an early reader, an uncle at eight years old, a camp counselor, a radio newscaster, a New York City tour guide, and an advertising creative director before contributing to the writing of this book.

Mark is a graduate of the University of Buffalo. He and his wife Kara live in New York.

Morten Kettel specializes in photographing people who want to be seen, places that want to be traveled to, and foods that want to be eaten.

Morten graduated from the Brooks Institute in Santa Barbara, California. He was born, raised, and still lives in the San Francisco Bay Area. He doesn't live in an orange building, either.